How to

swear & love

in

Dutch

Ingeborg Stinissen

How to swear and love in Dutch

Foreword

My dear friend,

First I want to thank a bunch of people who inspired me to write this book. I was on holiday in Ireland when I've met some women from America. Though I was the only European (Belgian) tourist at the time, I couldn't hold myself back teaching them a little bit from our lovely Dutch language. "Teach us all the bad stuff you know, in Dutch!" I wrote some stuff on a napkin and so it began. During the holiday they've put a smile on my face. Hilarious. Actually, instead of going on a holiday, I had to study for some finals. So I want to thank my parents too, for letting me go in the first place. I'm very grateful.

With love,

Ingeborg

Introduction: The Dutch alphabet

If you tried to pronounce my name, you already experienced some difficulties. You have to read it first, though. Well, things wouldn't go better when it comes to pronunciations. In Dutch, we use the letters of the alphabet a little bit in a different way. Let me enlighten you!

Letter	How to say it the Dutch way
A	Ah
B	Bai
C	Cai
D	Dai
E	Ai
F	Ef
G	Ghai (Soft 'g' at the back of your throat. This is where things go wrong)
H	Ha
I	Ee
J	Yai
K	Kha
L	El
M	Em
N	En
O	Oh
P	Pai
Q	Q
R	R (also back of the throat)

S	S
T	Tai
U	Uh
V	Vai
W	wai
X	X
Y	Ey
Z	zet

Numbers and figures

If you look at this table carefully, you see I don't know how to count properly. I was too lazy to write one billion numbers, so I suggested this will be far enough. You probably would skip this part anyway, lol. (Nope, I'm crying inside. All that work...Oh, my!)

1. one	één [ain]	10. ten	tien [teen]
2. two	Twee [twai]	20. twenty	twintig [twintəch]
3. three	drie [dree]	30. thirty	dertig [dertəch]
4. four	vier [veer]	40. forty	veertig [vairtəch]
5. five	vijf [veyf]	50. fifty	vijftig [veyftəch]
6. six	zes [zès]	60. sixty	zestig [zèstəch]
7. seven	zeven [zaivən]	70. seventy	zeventig (zaivəntəch]

8. eight	acht [acht]	80. eighty	tachtig [tachtəch]
9. nine	negen [naighən]	90. ninety	negentig [naigəntəch]
10. ten	tien [teen]	100. hundred	honderd [hondərt]
11. eleven	elf [elf]	21. twenty-one	één-en-twitintig [ain-en-twintəch]
12. twelve	twaalf [twaalf]	22. twenty-two	twee-en-twintig [twai-en-twintəch]
13. thirteen	dertien [derteen]	23. twenty-tree	drie-en-twintig [dree-en-twintəch]
14. fourteen	veertien [vairteen]	24. twenty-four	vier-en-twintig [veer-en-twintəch]
15. fifteen	vijftien [veyfteen]	25. twenty-five	vijf-en-twintig [veyf-en-twintəch]
16. sixteen	zestien [zèsteen]	26. twenty-six	zes-en-twintig [zès-en-twintəch]
17. seventeen	zeventien [zaivənteen]	27. twenty-seven	zeven-en-twintig [zaivən-en-twintəch]

5

18. eighteen	achttien [*achteen*]	**28. twenty-eight**	acht-en-twintig [*acht-en-twintəch*]
19. nineteen	negentien [*naigənteen*]	**29. twenty-nine**	negen-en-twintig [*naigən-en-twintəch*]
20. twenty	twintig [*twintəch*]	**30. thirty**	dertig [*dertəch*]
100. hundred	honderd [*hondərt*]	**1000. one thousand**	duizend [*duyzənt*]
101. one hundred-one	honderd-en-één [*hondərt-en-ain*]	**1001. one thousand and one**	duizend-en-één [*duyzənt-en-ain*]
110. one hundred-ten	honderd-en-tien [*hondərt-en-teen*]	**2000. two thousand**	tweeduizend [*twai duyzənt*]
121. one hundred twenty-one	honderd-een-en-twintig [*hondərt-ain-en-twintəch*]	**1,000,000. one million**	één miljoen [*ain milyoon*]
200. two hundred	tweehonderd [*twai-hondərt*]	**1,000,000,000. one billion**	één miljard [*ain milyard*]

But if you did look at the tables (I love you), you discovered an upside down 'e' (ə, see?) or schwa-symbol. It's not 'uh' or 'eh,' but something in between. Like 'deliver.' If you write it phonetically, you write 'delivər.' Looks pretty cool. Even if I read it myself.

True to life

Now we cleared that up; we're ready for the real work. How to use it in a sentence and in what situations can you say what? I picked the clichés among the clichés from the different stages of life. There will be things you recognize and some you don't. Nothing to be ashamed about.

I haven't mentioned it before, but the blue italic text is meant to be phonetic. I tried to make it readable for people who like to read things the English way. I'm terribly sorry if I give your tongue a hard time. (Wink!)

Meeting people

It's always nice to see how all countries introduce their self in their own way. In the part where I live, it's a little but unusual to say all these meeting-people-stuff. I think if you say 'hi' to a stranger, you're already a 'bit of a pervert in Belgium. Nothing to be ashamed about too. No, I'm exaggerating. I must say, I had to think hard to come up with something, but I managed to find some useful stuff!

1) Hi, my name is ...	Hallo, mijn naam is ... [Hallo, meyn naam is...]
2) What's your name?	Wat is uw naam? (formal) [Wat is uw naam?] Wat is jou naam? (informal) [Wat is yoaw naam?]
3) Can you spell that, please?	Kunt u dat spellen, alstublieft? (formal) [Kunt u dat spellən, alstubleeft?] Kun je dat spellen, alsjeblieft? (informal) [Kun yə dat spellən, alsyəbleeft?]

4) Nice to meet you.	Fijn u te ontmoeten. (formal) *[Feyn u tə ontmootən.]* Fijn je te ontmoeten. (informeel) *[Feyn yə tə ontmootən.]*
5) Where are you from?	Vanwaar bent u? *[Vahnwaar bent u?]*
6) Where do you live?	Waar woont u? *[Waar wohnt u?]*
7) I live in ...	Ik woon in ... *[Ek wohn in...]*
8) I am ... years old.	Ik ben ... jaar oud. *[Ek ben...yaar oath.]*
9) What's your address?	Wat is uw adres? (formal) [Wat is uw adres?] Wat is jou adres? (informal) *[Wat is yoaw adres?]*
10) Do you have a job?	Heeft u een job? *[Haift u ən job?]*
11) Where do you work?	Waar werkt u? *[Waar werkt u?]*
12) You work here?	Werkt u hier? *[Werkt u heer?]*

13) So, what do you do?	Zo, wat doet u? *[Zoh, waht doot u?]*
14) What brings you here?	Wat brengt u hier? *[Waht brengt u heer?]*
15) What was your name again?	Wat is uw naam weer? *[Waht is uw naam wair?]*
16) It was nice meeting you.	Het was fijn u te ontmoeten. *[Hət was feyn u tə ontmootən.]*
17) Goodbye!	Vaarwel! *[Vaarwel!]*
18) See you later.	Tot ziens. *[Tot zeens.]*

Flirting

The virtues of life. One of the few moments you forgot about your age, your work or the place you parked your car. Or was it called 'drunk'? Well, it doesn't matter anyway. Here you are! Ready to talk to that charming man or a lovely woman. The only thing you need is something to break the ice! Or you ask the nice bartender to crush it for you. It's up to you. Sorry, I was in the mood for a lame joke.

1) Do you come here often?	Kom je hier vaak? *[Kom yə heer vaak?]*
2) Did it hurt when you fell from heaven?	Deed het pijn toen je uit de hemel viel? *[Daid hət peyn toon yə uyt də haiməl veel?]*
3) I 'm writing a phone book. Can I have yours too?	Ik ben een telefoonboek aan het schrijven. Kan ik de jouwe ook hebben? *[Ek ben ən tailaiphohnbook aan hət schreyvən. Kan ek də yoawə ohk hebbən?]*
4) Can I have your number?	Kan ik jouw nummer hebben? *[Kahn ek yoaw nummər hebbən?]*

5)Would you like to go on a date with me?	Wil je eens met mij afspreken? *[Wil yə ains met mey afspraikən?]*
6) Would you like to see a movie sometime?	Wil je eens een film zien? *[Wil yə ains ən film zeen?]*
7) You have beautiful eyes.	Je hebt mooie ogen. *[Yə hebt mohyə ohgən.]*
8) I love your smile.	Ik houd van je lach. *[Ek how vahn yə lach.]*
9) You have nice glasses.	Je hebt een leuke bril. *[Yə hebt ən loikə bril.]*
10) I like you.	Ik vind jou leuk. *[Ek vind yoaw loik.]*
11) We could hang out sometime.	We zouden eens kunnen rondhangen. *[Wə zoadən ains kunnən rondhangən.]*
12)I would like to see you again.	Ik zou u graag willen terug zien. *[Ek zoaw u graach willən təruch zeen.]*
13) You have a very attractive voice.	Je hebt een heel aantrekkelijke stem. *[Yə hebt ən hail*

	aantrekkəleykə stem.]
14) You have a sexy accent.	Je hebt een sexy accent. *[Yə hebt ən sexy accent.]*
15) I'm an incredible kisser.	Ik ben een geweldige kusser. *[Ek ben ən gəweldigə kussər.]*

When flirting actually works

Well, If you want me to explain the title in a proper way, I will give you some hints. Wink! Though I must say that it feels a little awkward to write this part. I'm just aware of the fact that my mom could read this. On behave of myself: I'm sorry mom. Just skip a few chapters. For the rest of you sinful sinners: Well... Do whatever you like, honey.

1) Let's go to my place! (when you're convinced she/he 's going with you)	Laten we naar mijn plaats gaan! *[Laatən wə naar meyn plaats ghaan!]*
2) Let's go upstairs!	Laten we naar boven gaan! *[Laatən wə naar bohvən ghaan!]*

3) I want to kiss you.	Ik wil je kussen. *[Ek wil yə kussən.]*
4) I want to make love to you.	Ik wil met je vrijen. *[Ek wil met yə vreyən.]*
5) kiss me!	Kus me! *[Kus mə!]*
6) Are you sure you want to do this?	Ben je zeker dat je dit wil doen? *[Ben yə zaikər dat yə dit wil doon?]*
7) Do you have a condom with you?	Heb je een condoom bij? *[Heb yə ən condohm bey?]*
8) I forgot to bring one.	Ik vergat er een mee te nemen. *[Ek vərgat er ain mai tə naimən.]*
9) Do you take the pill?	Neem je de pil? *[Naim yə də pil?]*
10) I don't know what to do.	Ik weet niet wat ik moet doen. *[Ek wait neet waht ek moot doon.]*

11) I can't open your bra.	Ik kan je beha niet openen. *[Ek kahn yə baiha neet ohpənən.]*
12) I can't get it in. **(read: the key from the hotel door)**	Ik kan er niet in. *[Ek kahn er neet in.]*
13) Hold me!	Houd me vast! *[Hoad mə vahst!]*
14) Stay with me for a while!	Blijf bij me voor een tijdje! *[Bleyf bey mə vohr ən teydyə!]*
15) I don't regret it.	Ik heb er geen spijt van. *[Ek heb er gain speyt vahn.]*
16) I do regret it.	Ik heb er spijt van. *[Ek heb er speyt vahn.]*
17) We should do this more often.	We zouden dit vaker moeten doen. *[Wə zoadən dit vaakər mootən doon.]*

At the wedding

For some the most beautiful day in their life. For others a formality. It's always nice to see how people preserve some traditions of history. Think about it. How many years are we walking with a (white) dress to the altar? Not every wedding is the same of course, but the tasks of that day are pretty much comparable.

1) Do you have the rings?	Heeft u de ringen? *[Haift u də ringən?]*
2) Where are the rings?	Waar zijn de ringen? *[Waar zeyn də ringən?]*
3) I pronounce you husband and wife.	Ik verklaar u man en vrouw. *[Ek vərklaar u mahn en vroaw.]*
4) You may kiss the bride.	U mag de bruid kussen. *[U mach də bruyd kussən.]*
5) Take good care of my boy/girl!	Draag goed zorg voor mijn jongen/meisje! *[Draach good zorch vohr meyn yongən/meysyə!]*
6) I'll be watching you.	Ik houd je in de gaten. *[Ek hoad yə in də gaatən.]*

7) Can I steal your husband/wife for a second?	Kan ik je man/ vrouw even stelen? *[Kahn ek yə mahn/vroaw aivən stailən?]*
8) Did anybody see grandmother?	Heeft iemand oma gezien? *[Haift eemand omah gəzeen?]*
9) I have a few words for the couple.	Ik heb enkele woorden voor het koppel. *[Ek heb enkələ wohrdən vohr hət koppəl.]*
10) I give the marriage five years.	Ik geef het huwelijk vijf jaar. *[Ek gaif hət huwəleyk veyf yaar.]*
11) You're the worst best man I've known.	Je bent de slechtste getuige die ik ken. *[Yə bent də slechtstə gətuygə dee ek ken.]*
12) It was a beautiful ceremony.	Het was een prachtige ceremonie. *[Hət was ən prachtigə sairaimohnee.]*

Long term relationship

To be honest, I'm just suggesting what a regular couple would say to each other after the second date.

1) I love you.	Ik houd van jou. *[Ek hoaw vahn yoaw.]*
2) Do you want to marry me?	Wil je met me trouwen? *[Wil yə met mə troawən?]*
3) Do I look fat in these pants?	Zie ik er dik uit in deze broek? *[Zee ek er dik uyt in daizə brook?]*
4) Does my butt look fat in this dress?	Ziet mijn kont er dik uit in deze jurk? *[Zeet meyn kont er dik uyt in daizə yurk?]*
5) Why are you staring at her?	Waarom staar je naar haar? *[Waarom staar yə naar haar?]*
6) Why is he staring at you?	Waarom staart hij naar jou? *[Waarom staart hey naar yoaw?]*

7) You're blocking the television.	Je staat voor de televisie. *[Yǝ staat vohr dǝ tailaiveezee.]*
8) We should get a baby.	We zouden een baby moeten nemen. *[Wǝ zoadǝn ǝn baby mootǝn naimǝn.]*
9) We should get a dog.	We zouden een hond moeten nemen. *[Wǝ zoadǝn ǝn hond mootǝn naimǝn.]*
10) Did you lose weight?	Ben je afgevallen? *[Ben yǝ afgǝvahllǝn?]*
11) Did you gain weight?	Ben je bijgekomen? *[Ben yǝ beygǝkohmǝn?]*

On a diet

I think we live in a world today where we get an instant burnout when we hear somebody talk about diets. We are almost beaten 'till death by all the health commercials. But damn, why not? If it helps, it helps. You know, you wouldn't believe me. But trust me on this one: I've been on a diet more than ones. Wicked!

I know. So, here are a few examples I remembered from a previous or current life.

1) I will start tomorrow.	Ik zal morgen beginnen. *[Ek zahl morgən bəginnən.]*
2) I'm on a diet.	Ik ben op dieet. *[Ek ben op deeait.]*
3) I can eat anything I want.	Ik kan alles eten wat ik wil. *[Ek kahn alləs aitən waht ek wil.]*
4) I can't eat a damn thing.	Ik kan helemaal niets eten. *[Ek kahn hailəmaal neets aitən.]*
5) You're not supportive.	Je bent niet bemoedigend. *[Yə bent neet bəmoodigənd.]*
6) One piece couldn't harm anyone.	Een stukje kan geen kwaad. *[Ain stukyə kahn gain kwaad.]*
7) I need to open a few buttons.	Ik moet enkele knopen open doen. *[Ek moot enkələ knohpən*

opən doon.]

8) How much did you lose?	Hoeveel ben je afgevallen? *[Hoovail ben yə afgəvallən?]*
9) How much did you gain?	Hoeveel ben je bijgekomen? *[Hoovail ben yə beygəkohmən?]*
10) Can I have a diet coke with that?	Kan ik een light cola erbij krijgen? *[Kahn ek ən light cola erbey kreygən?]*
11) Did you workout?	Heb je getraind? *[Heb yə gətraind?]*
12) I can't lose weight because I'm going to have my period.	Ik kan niet afvallen, omdat ik ga menstrueren. *[Ek kahn neet afvallən, omdaht ek ga menstruairən.]*
13) I probably drank too much water.	Ik dronk vermoedelijk teveel water. *[Ek dronk vərmoodəleyk təvail watər.]*

Breaking up

Not the funniest thing to do. You can't find the right words or somewhat choose other ways to send the message. For those who are in the middle of a break-up: You are a strong man or woman. Better things are coming your way!

1) It's not what you think.	Het is niet wat je denkt. *[Hət is neet waht yə denkt.]*
2) It is what you think.	Het is wat je denkt. *[Hət is waht yə denkt.]*
3) It's not what it looks like.	Het is niet wat het lijkt. *[Hət is neet waht hət leykt.]*
4) It is what it looks like.	Het is wat het lijkt. *[Hət is waht hət leykt.]*
5) It's over between us.	Het is gedaan tussen ons. *[Hət is gədaan tussən ons.]*
6) This isn't going to work.	Dit gaat niet werken. *[Dit gaat neet werkən.]*
7) Are you breaking up with me?	Maak je het uit met mij? *[Maak yə hət uyt met mey?]*

8) I don't love you anymore.	Ik houd niet meer van jou. *[Ek hoaw neet mair vahn yoaw.]*
9) You never listen to me.	Je luistert nooit naar mij. *[Yə luystərt noyt naar mey.]*
10) I am taking the dog with me.	Ik neem de hond met me mee. *[Ek naim də hond met mə mai.]*
11) Don't call me again!	Bel me niet meer! *[Bel mə neet mair!]*
12) Why doesn't he/she call me?	Waarom belt hij/zij me niet? *[Waarom belt hey/zey mə neet?]*
13) It wasn't meant to be.	Het heeft niet mogen zijn. *[Hət haift neet mohgən zeyn.]*
14) We're running out of ice cream.	We hebben geen roomijs meer. *[Wə hebbən gain rohm-eys mair.]*

Being a tourist

Holidays are quite fun, are they? I personally love to travel. Seeing other places, people, more places, and other people. Nobody who annoys you or tells you what to do. Except for the people you travel with, probably. Otherwise, no strings attached. Enjoy life!

1) Could you tell me where I am?	Kunt u mij vertellen waar ik ben? (formal) *[Kunt u mey vərtellən waar ek ben?]* Kun je me vertellen waar ik ben? (informal) *[Kun yə mə vərtellən waar ek ben?]*
2) Could you help me find ...?	Kunt u me helpen... te vinden? *[Kunt u mə helpən...tə vindən?]*
3) Do you have a GPS-system on your cell phone?	Heeft u een GPS-systeem op uw gsm? *[Haift u ən GPS-seestaim op uw gsm?]*
4) I am lost.	Ik ben verloren. *[Ek ben vərlohrən.]*
5) Is this the hotel we're staying?	Is dit het hotel waarin we verblijven?

	[Is dit hət hotel waarin wə vərbleyvən?]
6) The room looked bigger on the internet.	De kamer leek groter op het internet. *[Də kaamər laik grohtər op hət intərnet.]*
7) The previous owners forgot their washcloth in the sink.	De vorige eigenaars vergaten hun washandje in de lavabo. *[Də vohrigə eygənaars vərgaatən hun washandyə in də laavaaboh.]*
8) I hope there's a lot to do around here.	Ik hoop dat hier een hoop te doen is. *[Ek hope daht heer ən hope tə doon is.]*
9) There is nothing to do around here.	Hier is niets te doen. *[Heer is neets tə doon.]*
10) I forgot my charger at home.	Ik vergat mijn lader thuis. *[Ek vərgat meyn laadər thuys.]*
11) What language do they speak over here?	Welke taal spreken ze hier? *[Welkə taal spraikən zə heer?]*

12) Did you understand them?	Heb jij hen verstaan? *[Heb yey hen vərstaan?]*
13) I can't communicate properly.	Ik kan niet deftig communiceren. *[Ek kahn neet deftich communeesairən.]*
14) That was probably an important statue.	Dat was vermoedelijk een belangrijk standbeeld. *[Daht wahs vərmoodəleyk ən bəlangreyk stahndbaild.]*
15) Let's go home!	Laten we naar huis gaan! *[Laatən wə naar huys gaan!]*
16) I want to stay a little bit longer.	Ik wil een klein beetje langer blijven. *[Ik wil ən kleyn baityə langər bleyvən.]*

At the restaurant

Yeah... I'm going to get myself some food. Keep up the reading!

1) Can I have a table, please?	Kan ik een tafel krijgen, alstublieft? *[Kahn ek ən taafəl kreygən, alstubleeft?]*
2) Can we order, please?	Kunnen we bestellen, alstublieft? *[Kunnən wə bəstellən, alstubleeft?]*
3) I didn't order this.	Dit heb ik niet besteld. *[Dit heb ek neet bəsteld.]*
4) Waiter!	Ober! *[Ohbər!]*
5) I have a hair in my soup.	Ik heb een haar in mijn soep. *[Ek heb ən haar in meyn soop.]*
6) Can I eat this with my hands?	Kan ik dit eten met mijn handen? *[Kahn ek dit aitən met meyn handən?]*

7) Can I pay the bill, please?	Kan ik de rekening betalen, alstublieft? *[Kahn ek də raikəning bətaalən, alstubleeft?]*
8) I can't read the menu.	Ik kan de menu-kaart niet lezen. *[Ek kahn də mənu-kaart neet laizən.]*
9) Do you have white toast?	Heeft u wit geroosterd brood? *[Haift u wit gərohstərd brohd?]*
10) Can we get another table, please?	Kunnen we een andere tafel krijgen, alstublieft? *[Kunnən wə ən andərə taafəl kreygən, alstubleeft?]*
11) Don't you need to powder your nose?	Moet je je neus niet poederen? *[Moot yə yə nois neet poodərən?]*
12) I like the food.	Ik houd van het eten. *[Ek hoaw vahn hət aitən.]*
13) I adore the food.	Ik adoreer het eten. *[Ek aadohrair hət aitən.]*

14) Bring me the best wine you have!	Breng me de beste wijn die je hebt! *[Breng mə də bestə weyn dee yə hebt!]*
15) I suppose I can't smoke up here?	Ik veronderstel dat ik hier niet kan roken? *[Ek vərondərstel daht ek heer neet kahn rohkən?]*
16) Do you know where I can find a toilet here?	Weet u waar ik hier een toilet kan vinden? *[Wait u waar ik heer ən twaalet kahn vindən?]*

At the pub

The pub. One of the rare things that survived in history. A point where people gather around to enjoy themselves. A place where the level of conversations reaches a higher state, after a few drinks. A place to love and maybe cry.

1) It smells in here.	Het stinkt hier. *[Hət stinkt heer.]*
2) Give the man a beer, would you?	Geef de man een bier, wil je? *[Gaif də mahn ən beer, wil yə?]*

3) I'm not drunk.	Ik ben niet dronken. *[Ek ben neet dronkən.]*
4) I have to go outside.	Ik moet naar buiten gaan. *[Ek moot naar buytən gaan.]*
5) I think she/he likes me.	Ik denk dat zij/hij me leuk vindt. *[Ek denk daht zey/hey mə loik vind.]*
6) I'll go for another round.	Ik ga voor nog een rondje. *[Ek gaa vohr noch ən rondyə.]*
7) I'll stop drinking tomorrow.	Ik zal morgen stoppen met drinken. *[Ek zahl morgən stoppən met drinkən.]*
8) Are you drunk?	Ben je dronken? *[Ben yə dronkən?]*
9) I'm a little tipsy.	Ik ben een beetje aangeschoten. *[Ek ben ən baityə aangəschohtən.]*
10) Do you know where I parked the car?	Weet jij waar ik de auto geparkeerd heb? *[Wait yey waar ek də*

| 11) I can't feel my shoe. | Ik kan mijn schoen niet voelen. *[Ek kahn meyn schoon neet voolən.]* |

| 12) I'm able to drive. | Ik ben in staat om te rijden. *[Ek ben in staat om tə reydən.]* |

| 13) I'll marry the bartender. | Ik zal met de barman trouwen. *[Ek zahl met də barmahn traowən.]* |

When you don't like that person at that particular moment

However, I take full responsibility by teaching you the following slang (Forget what I've said! It felt wonderful.) I must insist that you use these words in moderation.

| 1) Eat shit! | Eet stront! *[Ait stront!]* |

2) Asshole	Smeerlap
	[Smairlap]
3) Simple mind	Onnozelaar
	[Onnohzəlaar]
4) I don't like you.	Ik vind je niet leuk.
	[Ek vind yə neet loik.]
5) Get lost!	Flikker op!
	[Flikkər op!]
	Loop naar de pomp!
	[Lohp naar də pomp!]
	(literal translation: Run to the pump!)
	Loop naar de maan!
	[Lohp naar də maan!]
	(literal translation: Run to the moon!)
6) You're annoying.	Je bent vervelend.
	[Yə bent vərvailənd.]
7) What are you staring at?	Waar staar je naar?
	[Waar staar yə naar?]
8) Simpleton	Dommerik
	[Dommərik]
9) Talk to the hand!	Praat tegen de hand!
	[Praat taigən də hahnd!]

10) Cobblers	Onzin
	[Onzin]
11) Are you still here?	Ben je nog steeds hier?
	[Ben yə nog staids heer?]
12) Asscracker	Kontbeschuit
	[Kontbəschuyt]
13) You're an ass.	Je bent een idioot.
	[Yə bent ən eedee-oht.]
14) Retarded idiot	Achterlijke idioot
	[Achtərleykə eedee-oht]
15) Moron	Debiel
	[Daibeel]

At a job interview

Getting a job. A time to conquer doubt. A time where you try to make yourself feel better, by giving your mirror compliments. A time where you nervously replaced you drunk pictures on social media with one on an expensive party, with an awkward grin. A time that I never will experience after writing this book. A time of pain and misery. Let's go on with our list, shall we?

1) What are your qualities?	Wat zijn uw kwaliteiten? *[Waht zeyn uw kwaaleeteytən?]*
2) What are your weak points?	Wat zijn uw zwakke punten? *[Waht zeyn uw zwakkə puntən?]*
3) Do you have experience in this field?	Heeft u ervaring in dit veld? *[Haift u ervahring in dit veld?]*
4) What did you do the last two years?	Wat heeft u de laatste twee jaar gedaan? *[Waht haift u də laatstə twai yaar gədaan?]*
5) Where do you see yourself in five years?	Waar ziet u uzelf in vijf jaar? *[Waar zeet u uzelf in veyf yaar?]*
6) Do you like to travel?	Vindt u reizen leuk? *[Vind u reyzən loik?]*
7) Do you mind being away from home for a while?	Vindt u het erg om een tijdje van huis weg te zijn? *[Vind u hət erg om ən teydyə vahn huys weg tə zeyn?]*

8) You're the man/woman we're looking for!	U bent de man/ vrouw die we zoeken! *[U bent də mahn/ vroaw dee wə zookən!]*

9) I'm the man/woman you're looking for!	Ik ben de man/ vrouw die u zoekt! *[Ek ben də mahn/ vroaw dee u zookt!]*

10) We think you don't have enough experience.	We denken dat u niet genoeg ervaring heeft. *[Wə denkən dat u neet gənooch ervaaring haift.]*

11) We will call you back.	We zullen u terug bellen. *[Wə zullən u təruch bellən.]*

At work

Having the job. Oh wow. Don't know what to say about this chapter, though. For those who do it: You're brave!

1) It was already like this when I came in.	Het was al zo toen ik binnenkwam. *[Hət was ahl zoh toon ek bInnənkwam.]*

2) It wasn't like this when I left.	Het was niet zo, toen ik vertrok. *[Hət was neet zoh, toon ek vərtrok.]*
3) It wasn't me.	Ik was het niet. *[Ek was hət neet.]*
4) The boss is looking in our direction.	De baas is in onze richting aan het kijken. *[Də baas is in onzə richting aan hət keyken.]*
5) We better go back to work.	We kunnen beter terug aan het werk gaan. *[Wə kunnən baitər təruch aan hət werk gaan.]*
6) Can I get a raise?	Kan ik opslag krijgen? *[Kahn ek opslach kreygən?]*
7) Are you firing me?	Bent u mij aan het ontslaan? *[Bent u mey aan hət ontslaan?]*
8) You're getting a promotion.	U krijgt een promotie. *[U kreycht ən promosee.]*
9) You're fired!	U bent ontslagen! *[U bent ontslaagən!]*

10) I'm counting on you.	Ik reken op u.
	[Ek raikən op u.]
11) The boss likes you.	De baas vindt u leuk.
	[Də baas vind u loik.]
12) The boss doesn't like you.	De baas vindt u niet leuk.
	[Də baas vind u neet loik.]
13) I'm leaving this place.	Ik verlaat deze plek.
	[Ek vərlaat daizə plek.]
14) Don't you dare quit!	Waag het niet te stoppen!
	[Waach hət neet tə stoppən!]
15) You have to earn your spot.	U moet uw plek verdienen.
	[U moot uw plek vərdeenən.]
16) Time is money.	Tijd is geld.
	[Teyd is geld.]
17) Now we're talking business.	Nu praten we over zaken.
	[Nu praatən wə ovər zaakən.]
18) I don't like your attitude.	Ik vind uw houding niet leuk.
	[Ek vind uw hoading neet loik.]

19) You got to think big.	U moet groot denken.
	[U moot groht denkən.]
20) You cost our company a lot of money.	U kost ons bedrijf een hoop geld.
	[U kost ons bədreyf ən hohp geld.]
21) How do you feel about retirement?	Hoe voelt u zich over pensioen?
	[Hoo voolt u zich ovər pensyoon?]

On the road

On the road. Ready to go to work, vacation or people you promised to visit finally. I must think about the frustrating traffic these days. Lots of cars which have to be at the same location at the same time. Although I don't own a drivers license at this particular moment, I feel for everybody who has to deal with this issue more often.

1) We're stuck in traffic.	We zitten vast in het verkeer.
	[Wə zittən vahst in hət vərkair.]
2) It was a red light.	Het was rood licht.
	[Hət was rohd licht.]

3) It was a green light.	Het was groen licht. *[Hət was groon licht.]*
4) It was yellow light.	Het was oranje licht. *[Hət was oranyə licht.]*
5) You drive too fast.	Je rijdt te snel. *[Yə reyd tə snel.]*
6) You drive too slow.	Je rijdt te traag. *[Yə reyd tə traach.]*
7) I think we have a flat tire.	Ik denk dat we een platte band hebben. *[Ek denk daht wə ən plattə bahnd hebbən.]*
8) We took the wrong turn.	We namen de verkeerde afslag. *[Wə naamən də vərkairdə afslach.]*
9) You gave me the wrong address.	Je gaf me het verkeerde adres. *[Yə gahf mə hət vərkairdə ahdres.]*
10) Don't yell at me!	Schreeuw niet tegen mij! *[Schraiw neet taigən mey!]*
11) Did we hit anything?	Hebben we iets geraakt? *[Hebbən wə eets*

12) What did the GPS-system say?	Wat heeft het GPS-systeem gezegd? *[Wat haift hət GPS-seestaim gəzechd?]*
13) It's slippery on the road.	Het is glad op de weg. *[Hət is glahd op də wech.]*
14) I hope we aren't flashed.	Ik hoop dat we niet geflitst zijn. *[Ek hohp daht wə neet gəflitst zeyn.]*
15) I wish we had a bigger car.	Ik wenste dat we een grotere wagen hadden. *[Ek wenstə daht wə ən grohtərə waagən haddən]*
16) I wish we had a smaller car.	Ik wenste dat we een kleinere wagen hadden. *[Ek wenstə daht wə ən kleynərə waagən haddən.]*
17) Why did he stop in front of us?	Waarom stopte hij voor ons? *[Waarom stoptə hey vohr ons?]*

18) Keep driving!	Blijf rijden! *[Bleyf reydən!]*
19) I just saw an accident.	Ik zag net een ongeluk. *[Ek zach net ən ongəluk.]*
20) You will get us killed.	Je jaagt ons de dood in. *[Yə yaacht ons də dohd in.]*
21) Did someone just farted in here?	Heeft hier iemand een scheet gelaten? *[Haift heer eemand ən schait gəlaatən?]*
22) Pull down the window, honey.	Doe het raam omlaag, lieverd. *[Doo hət raam omlaach, leevərd.]*
23) I'm going to buy myself a motorcycle.	Ik ga mezelf een motor kopen. *[Ek gaa məzelf ən motor kopən.]*
24) You're better off taking the train.	Je bent beter af als je de trein neemt. *[Yə bent baitər af als yə də treyn naimt.]*
25) I'm going to stay home next time.	Ik blijf de volgende keer thuis. *[Ek bleyf də volgəndə kair thuyɛ.]*

Being polite

Well, I'm stuck. Politeness...Feels like a rare thing these days. Although people feel more respected and valuable if you use it more often. I speak for myself, though. It's a skill what makes you more attractive. But don't overdo it. You got to keep the conversation real and easygoing.

1) Have a nice day!	Fijne dag! *[Feynə dach!]*
2) Take your time!	Neem je tijd! *[Naim yə teyd!]*
3) I'm not in a rush.	Ik heb geen haast. *[Ek heb gain haast.]*
4) Please	Alstublieft *[Alstubleeft]*
5) That's awful. (replacement for unnecessary emotional questions)	Dat is verschrikkelijk. *[Daht is vərschrikkəleyk.]*
6) I'll keep the door open.	Ik zal de deur open houden. *[Ek zahl də doir opən hoadən.]*
7) Let me introduce you to...	Laat me u voorstellen aan...

	[Laat mə u vohrstellən aan...]
8) I don't want to be rude, but...	Ik wil niet onbeleeft zijn, maar... *[Ek wil neet onbəlaift zeyn, maar...]*
9) How can I help you today?	Hoe kan ik u helpen vandaag? *[Hoo kahn ek u helpən vahndaach?]*
10) I think you're very kind.	Ik denk dat u zeer vriendelijk bent. *[Ek denk daht u zair vreendəleyk bent.]*

Special holidays and stuff

I'll mention holidays which pop in my mind or on the internet. You know, there are a lot of different countries around. All those countries have a lot of holidays on their own. If yours not in it, I'm terribly sorry. So, without offending someone: Here you go.

1) Happy birthday!	Gelukkige verjaardag! *[Gəlukkigə vəryaardach!]*

2) **Happy Thanksgiving!**	Gelukkige Dankdag!
	[Gəlukkigə Dahnkdach!]
3) **Happy Newyear!**	Gelukkig Nieuwjaar!
	[Gəlukkich Neewyaar!]
4) **Valentine's Day**	Valentijnsdag
	[Vaaləteynsdach]
5) **Presidents' Day**	Presidentendag
	[Praiseedentəndach]
6) **Easter**	Pasen
	[Paasən]
7) **Mothers' Day**	Moederdag
	[Moodərdach]
8) **Memorial Day**	Herdenkingsdag
	[Herdenkingsdach]
9) **Fathers' Day**	Vaderdag
	[Vaadərdach]
10) **Independence Day**	Onafhankelijkheidsdag
	[Onafhankəleykheydsdach]
11) **Labor Day**	Dag van de Arbeid
	[Dach vahn də Arbeyd]
12) **Halloween**	Halloween

	[Halloween]
13) Veterans Day	Veteranendag
	[Vaitairaanəndach]
14) Merry Christmas!	Vrolijk Kerstfeest!
	[Vrohlək Kerstfaist!]
15) International Woman's Day	Internationale Vrouwendag
	[Intərnahtiohnaalə Vroawəndach]
16) International Man's Day	Internationale Mannendag
	[Intərnahtiohnaalə Mahnnəndach]
17) New Years' Eve	Oudejaarsavond
	[Oadəyaarsaavond]
18) Employee Day	Werknemersdag
	[Werknaimərsdach]
19) Boss Day	Baasdag
	[Baasdach]
20) World Peace Day	Wereld Vrededag
	[Wairəld Vraidədach]
21) Republic Day	Dag van de Republiek
	[Dach vahn də Raipubleek]
22) Sint Patrick's Day	Sint Patrickdag
	[Sint Patrickdach]

23) Youth Day	Jeugddag *[Yoichddach]*
24) World Frog Day	Wereld Kikkerdag *[Wairəld Kikkərdach]*
25) World Turtle Day	Wereld Schildpaddendag *[Wairəld Schildpaddəndach]*

Dutch proverbs

Like everywhere, we use different proverbs. I thought it would be funny to give the literal versions of our proverbs. Things couldn't make more sense, do they?

1) Als de kat van huis is, dansen de muizen op tafel. *[Als də kat vahn huys is, dansən də muyzən op taafəl.]*	Literally: When the cat's away from home, the mice will play. Meaning: When the boss is away, fun will start among the colleagues.
2) Al draagt de aap een gouden ring, het is en blijft een lelijk ding. *[Al draacht də aap ən goadən ring, hət is en bleyft ən laileyk ding.]*	Literally: Even if the monkey wears a golden ring, it is and stays an ugly thing. Meaning: You can't cover an ugly personality with nice clothes.

3) De appel valt niet ver van de boom. *[Də appəl valt neet ver vahn də bohm.]*	Literally: The apple doesn't fall far from the tree. Meaning: People almost do act the same way like their parents.
4) Wiens brood men eet, diens woord men spreekt. *[Weens brohd men ait, deens wohrd men spraikt.]*	Literally: Whose bread men eat, whose word men speak. Meaning: You have to listen to the person who depends on livelihood.
5) Pluk de dag. *[Pluk də dach.]*	Literally: Seize the day Meaning: Enjoy today.
6) Al doende leert men. *[Al doondə lairt men.]*	Literally: Practise makes perfect. Meaning: If you do something often, you eventually learn how to do it right.
7) Eerlijkheid duurt het langst. *[Airləkheyd duurt hət langst.]*	Literally: Honesty takes the longest. Meaning: The advantage you think to have from lying, won't last forever.

8) Een ezel stoot zich geen tweemaal aan dezelfde steen.
[ən aizəl stoht zich gain twaimaal aan dəzelfdə stain.]

Literally: The donkey doesn't strike the same rock twice.
Meaning: You (regularly) don't make the same mistake twice.

9) Wie goed doet, goed ontmoet.
[Wee good doot, good ontmoot.]

Literally: Who good does, good meet.
Meaning: Who helps another person, will be treated kindly.

10) Het gras is altijd groener aan de overkant.
[Hət gras is alteyd groonər aan də ohvərkant.]

Literally: The grass is always greener on the other side.
Meaning: You always want what someone else has.

11) Vele handen maken licht werk.
[Vaile handən maakən licht werk.]

Literally: Lot's of hands make lighter work.
Meaning: A bigger task is quicker done by a lot of people.

12) Uit het oog, uit het hart.
[Uyt hət ohg, uyt hət hart.]

Literally: Out of the eye, out of the heart.
Meaning: You will lose someone's attention if the person's not near you for a while.

13) Blaffende honden bijten niet. *[Blaffəndə hondən beytən neet.]*	Literally: Barking dogs don't bite. Meaning: If someone threatens you with something, doesn't mean he/she will fulfill the threat.
14) Van dik hout zaagt men planken. *[Vahn dik hoat zaacht men plankən.]*	Literally: From thick wood people cut planks. Meaning: Pushy work will not bring accurate results.
15) Ieder huisje heeft zijn kruisje. *[Eedər huysyə haift zeyn kruysyə.]*	Literally: Every home has his cross. Meaning: Everywhere is something wrong.
16) Men moet het ijzer smeden als het heet is. *[Men moot hət eyzər smaidən als hət hait is.]*	Literally: One should hammer the iron while it's hot. Meaning: Acting when the opportunity is there.
17) Jong geleerd, oud gedaan. *[Yong gəlaird, oad gədaan.]*	Literally: Learned young, old done. Meaning: The skills people learn while they're young, they still remember when they're old.

18) De kleren maken de man. *[Də klairən maakən də man.]*	Literally: The clothes make the man. Meaning: A person's clothing determines the respect he/she gets.
19) Zoals het klokje thuis tikt, tikt het nergens. *[Zoh-als hət klokyə thuys tikt, tikt hət nergəns.]*	Literally: Like the clock ticks at home, it ticks nowhere else. Meaning: It's nowhere as good as home.
20) Een dag niet gelachen, is een dag niet geleefd. *[ən dach neet gəlachən, is ən dach neet gəlaifd.]*	Literally: A day without laughter, is a day not alive. Meaning: Every day you should be at least happy once.
21) Lekker is maar één vinger lang. *[Lekkər is maar ain vingər lang.]*	Literally: Yummy is just one finger long. Meaning: Superficial pleasures just give relative satisfaction.
22) Zolang er leven is, is er hoop. *[Zohlang er laivən is, is er hohp.]*	Literally: When there's life, there is hope. Meaning: How bad circumstances are; if not everything is lost, everything is going to be all right.

23) De laatste loodjes wegen het zwaarst.
[Də laatstə lohdyəs waigən hət zwaarst.]

Literally: The final work weighs the heaviest.
Meaning: The end of the task seems more difficult than the beginning.

24) Als de maan vol is, schijnt ze overal.
[Als də maan vol is, scheynt zə ohvəral.]

Literally: When the moon is full, she shines everywhere.
Meaning: Everyone can see it when someone's happy.

25) Dat is mosterd na de maaltijd.
[Daht is mostərd naa də maalteyd.]

Literally: That's mustard after the meal.
Meaning: Relates to a comment that was made too late.

26) Als de nood het hoogst is, is de redding nabij.
[Als də nohd hət hochst is, is də reddingnaabey.]

Literally: When the need is high, salvation is near.
Meaning: If you are most in need of something, it will not take long before it's present.

27) Onbekend maakt onbemind.
[Onbəkend maakt onbəmind.]

Literally: Unknown makes unloved.
Meaning: Something few people know, is wrongly too little appreciated.

28) Overdaad schaadt. *[Ohvərdaad schaad.]*	Literally: Supererogation damages. Meaning: Too much is bad.
29) Naar iemands pijpen dansen. *[Naar eemands peypən dansən.]*	Literally: Dance to someone's trousers. Meaning: Do what someone dictates.
30) De uitzondering bevestigt de regel. *[Də uytzondəring bəvesticht də raigəl.]*	Literally: The exception confirms the rule. Meaning: There are exceptions everywhere.

Some quotes to think about

You know, I was writing a few quotes earlier on. Because I'm easily distracted, I took a break after two quotes. During my 'break' I've read a few articles. One of them was a Belgian article (of course) about posting quotes on social media and the fact you would have a low IQ, if you regularly participate on that matter. I must say I was a little bit offended. Good for me I put it in a book. I'm smart.

1) "I don't think anyone has a normal family."	"ik denk dat niemand een normale familie heeft."

- Edward Furlong	*[Ek denk daht neemand ən normaalə fahmeelee haift.]*
2) "Believe that life is worth living, and your believe will help create the fact." **- William James**	"Geloof dat leven de moeite waard is, en je geloof zal het feit creëren." *[Gəlohf daht laivən də mooytə waard is, en yə gəlohf zahl hət feyt crai-airən.]*
3) "One loyal friend is worth ten thousand relatives." **- Euripides**	"Eén loyale vriend is tien duizend verwanten waard." *[Ain loyaalə vreend is teen duyzənd vərwantən waard.]*
4) " A single rose can be my garden...a single friend, my world." **- Leo Buscaglia**	"Een enkele roos kan mijn tuin zijn... een enkele vriend, mijn wereld." *[ən enkələ rohs kahn meyn tuyn zeyn... ən enkələ vreend, meyn wairəld.]*
5) "Be miserable. Or motivate yourself. Whatever has to be done, it's always your	"Wees ellendig. Of motiveer jezelf. Wat moet gedaan worden, het is altijd jouw keuze."

choice." - Wayne Dyer	*[Wais ellendich. Of mohteevair yəzelf. Waht moot gədaan wordən, hət is alteyd yoaw koizə.]*
6) "It's pretty hard to tell what does bring happiness; poverty and wealth have both failed." - Kin Hubbard	"Het is moeilijk te vertellen wat geluk brengt. Armoede en rijkdom hebben beide gefaald." *[Hət is mooyleyk tə vərtellən waht gəluk brengt. Armoodə en reykdom hebbən beydə gəfaald.]*
7) "Too much tv hurts movies." - Elvis Presley	"Te veel tv kwetst films." *[Tə vail taivai kwetst films.]*
8) "Try to be like the turtle: at ease in your own shell." - Bill Copeland	"Probeer om als de schildpad te zijn: Op je gemak in je eigen schulp." *[Probair om als də schildpad tə zeyn: op yə gəmak in yə eygen schulp.]*
9) "The best way to predict the future is to invent it."	"De beste manier om de toekomst te voorspellen is om ze uit te vinden."

- Alan Kay	*[Də bestə mahneer om də tookomst tə vohrspellən is om zə uyt tə vindən.]*
10) "Rarely do members of the same family grow up under the same roof." - Richard Bach	"Zelden groeien leden van dezelfde familie op onder één dak." *[Zeldən grooyən laidən vahn dəzelfdə faameelee ondər ain dahk.]*
11) "Life is a dream for the wise, a game for the fool, a comedy for the rich, a tragedy for the poor." - Sholom Aleichem	"Het leven is een droom voor de wijzen, een spel voor de onnozele, een komedie voor de rijken, een tragedie voor de armen." *[Hət laivən is ən drohm vohr də weyzən, ən spel vohr də onnozələ, ən komaidee vohr də reykən, ən trachaidee vohr də armən.]*
12) "Assumptions are the termites of relationships." - Henry Winkler	"Veronderstellingen zijn de termieten van relaties." *[Vərondərstellingən zeyn də termeetən vahn railaasees.]*
13) "Friends and good manners will carry you	"Vrienden en goede manieren dragen u waar

where money won't go." **- Margaret Walker**	geld niet naartoe gaat." *[Vreendən en goodə* *mahneerən draachən u* *waar geld neet naartoo* *gaat.]*
14) "Well done is better **than well said."** **- Benjamin Franklin**	"Goed gedaan is beter dan goed gezegd." *[Good gədaan is baitər* *dan good gəzechd.]*
15) "Happiness is not a **goal; it is a by-product."** **-Eleanor Roosevelt**	"Geluk is geen doel; het is een bij-product." *[Gəluk is gain dool; hət is* *ən bey-product.]*
16) "A film is a petrified **fountain of thought."** **- Jean Cocteau**	"Een film is een versteende fontein van gedachten." *[ən film is ən vərstaində* *fonteyn vahn gədachtən.]*
17) "We can't help **everyone, but everyone** **can help someone."** **- Ronald Reagan**	"We kunnen niet iedereen helpen, maar iedereen kan iemand helpen." *[Wə kunnən neet* *eedərain helpən, maar* *eedərain kahn eemand* *helpən.]*
18) "It's not what you **look at that matters, it's** **what you see."**	"Het is niet naar wat je kijkt dat telt, het is wat je ziet."

- Henry David Thoreau

[Hət is neet naar wat yə keykt dat telt, hət is wat yə zeet.]

19) "I believe the world is one big family, and we need to help each other."
- Jet Li

"Ik geloof dat de wereld één grote familie is, en dat we elkaar moeten helpen."
[Ek gəlohf daht də wairəld ain grohtə faameelee is, en daht wə elkaar mootən helpən.]

20) "Every man dies. Not every man really lives."
- William Wallace

"Iedere man sterft. Niet elke man leeft echt."
[Eedərə man sterft. Neet elkə man laift echt.]

21) "Relationships based on obligation lack dignity."
- Wayne Dyer

"Relaties gebaseerd op verplichting ontbreken waardigheid."
[Railaatees gəbaasaird op vərplichting ontbraikən waardigheyd.]

22) "A true friend is someone who is there for you when he'd rather be anywhere else."
- Len Wein

"Een echte vriend is iemand die er voor je is, terwijl hij liever ergens anders zou willen zijn."
[ən echtə vreend is eemand dee er vohr yə is, terweyl hey leevər ergəns andərs zoaw willən zeyn.]

23) "If you don't like how things are, change it! You're not a tree." - Jim Rohn	"Als je het niet leuk vindt hoe dingen zijn, verander het! Je bent geen boom." *[Als yə hət neet loik vind hoo dingən zeyn, vərandər hət! Yə bent gain bohm.]*
24) "Happiness is like a kiss. You must share it to enjoy it." - Bernard Meltzer	"Geluk is zoals een kus. Je moet het delen om ervan te genieten." *[Gəluk is zoh-ahls ən kus. Yə moot hət dailən om ervahn tə gəneetən.]*
25) "The secret to film is that's it's an illusion." - George Lucas	"Het geheim van film is dat het een illusie is." *[Hət gəheym vahn film is daht hət ən illusee is.]*
26) "It is always the simple that produces the marvellous." - Amelia Barr	"Het is altijd het eenvoudige dat het wonderbaarlijke produceert." *[Hət is alteyd hət ainvoadigə daht hət wondərbaarleykə prohdusairt.]*
27) "True knowledge exists in knowing that you know nothing." - Socrates	"Ware kennis bestaat in de wetenschap dat je niets weet." *[Waarə kennis bəstaat in*

də waitənschap daht yə
neets wait.]

28) "When we remember we are all mad, the mysteries disappear and life stands explained."
- Mark Twain

"Als we bedenken dat we allemaal gek zijn, verdwijnen de mysteries en het leven wordt uitgelicht."
[Als wə bədenkən daht wə alləmaal gek zeyn, vərdweynən də mysteries en hət laiven word uytgəlicht.]

29) "Problems are not stop signs, they are guidelines."
- Robert H. Schuller

"Problemen zijn geen stopsignalen, het zijn richtlijnen."
[Problaimən zeyn gain stopsignaalən, hət zeyn richtleynən.]

30) "If it were not for hopes, the heart would break."
- Thomas Fuller

"Als het niet voor hoop was, zou het hart breken."
[Als hət neet vohr hohp was, zoaw hət hart braikən.]

Thank you for reading this, until the last page. I love you.

Tot Ziens!

12121159R00035

Printed in Great Britain
by Amazon